Around Town

Chris K. Soentpiet

LOTHROP, LEE & SHEPARD BOOKS   NEW YORK

Some people live in the country,
  where there are horses and big fields to play in.
Some people live at the seashore,
  where they stay wet on hot summer days.
Some people live in the suburbs,
  where there are shopping malls and backyard picnics.
But some people live in the city,
  where houses are built close together
  and backyards are tiny
  and streets are always busy,
  and where sometimes it feels
  like there's everything under the sun.

Cities have hydrants for hot summer days,

and toy shops right on the sidewalks.

Cities hide railroads under their streets,

BUSKER is an old
English word for a
person who entertains
by Singing in the
street for TIPS

and people play games on top of the trains.

Cities have picnics on tables with cloths,

and millions of birds to eat what you didn't.

They even have horses!

A city on a summer Saturday is like a country county fair,
with puppets and balloons,

and jugglers,

and people to draw your picture,

and others to paint your face.

And when you are tired at the end of the day,
a city can rub that tiredness right out of you,

CHINESE HERBAL MEDICINE feels oh so good!

and even fix your shoe.
All of it there right on the street,
without ever stepping inside a door.

Some people live in the country
    or at the seashore
    or in the suburbs,
and lots of those people don't like a city.
But some people live in the city
    and think it's the best place of all.

TO TED AND BETSY LEWIN
THANKS FOR YOUR WONDERFUL HELP AND GUIDANCE
and thanks to Susan and Rachel

First Edition 1 2 3 4 5 6 7 8 9 10

Library of Congress Cataloging in Publication
Soentpiet, Chris K.   Around town / by Chris K. Soentpiet.
p.   cm.   ISBN 0-688-04572-3. — ISBN 0-688-04573-1 (lib. bdg.)   1. City and town
life — Pictorial works — Juvenile literature.   2. Cities and towns — Pictorial works — Juvenile
literature.   [1. City and town life.   2. Cities and towns.]   I. Title.   HT119.S64   1994
307.76 — dc20   93-23519   CIP   AC